STEP-BY-STEP™
DRAW
HORSES

MARK BERGIN

BOOK HOUSE

This edition first published in MMXVII by
Book House

Distributed by Black Rabbit Books
P.O. Box 3263
Mankato
Minnesota MN 56002

Cataloging-in-Publication Data is available
from the Library of Congress

Printed in the United States
At Corporate Graphics,
North Mankato, Minnesota

9 8 7 6 5 4 3 2 1

ISBN: 978-1-911242-23-9

CONTENTS

MAKING A START

There are many different types of horses and ponies to draw. You can practice drawing horses from real life or from photographs. You can also use mannequin models or statues to practice poses. In these basic sketches, you can see how using construction lines can help you draw difficult parts of the horse's body and head.

4

Remember that practice makes
perfect. If a drawing doesn't
look right, start again and
keep working at it.

DRAWING MATERIALS

There are many different ways to approach a drawing. Try different materials such as pencils, pen and ink, brush pens, felt-tip pens, and colored pencils. Each creates quite a different result that will add variety to your drawings.

Felt-tips come in a range of line widths. The broader tips are good for filling in large areas of flat tone, as in a silhouette.

It can be tricky adding light and shade with an **ink** pen. Analyze your drawing. The lightest areas should be left untouched. Then apply solid areas of ink to the darkest parts. The midtones are achieved by hatching (single parallel lines) or cross–hatching (criss–crossed lines).

Hard pencils are more grey and soft pencils are blacker. Hard pencils are graded from 6H (the hardest) through 5H, 4H, 3H, 2H, and H.

Soft pencils are graded from B, 2B, 3B, 4B, 5B, and up to 6B (the softest).

7

CONSTRUCTION MARKS

By using circles and simple shapes you can practice drawing horses in any position. It's a quick and easy approach to capture a horse's shape and movement.

Draw circular shapes for the main features of the horse: the muzzle, the head, the front and rear body, the knees and ankle joints.

Draw in lines to connect these main sections to create the shape of the horse.

9

PERSPECTIVE

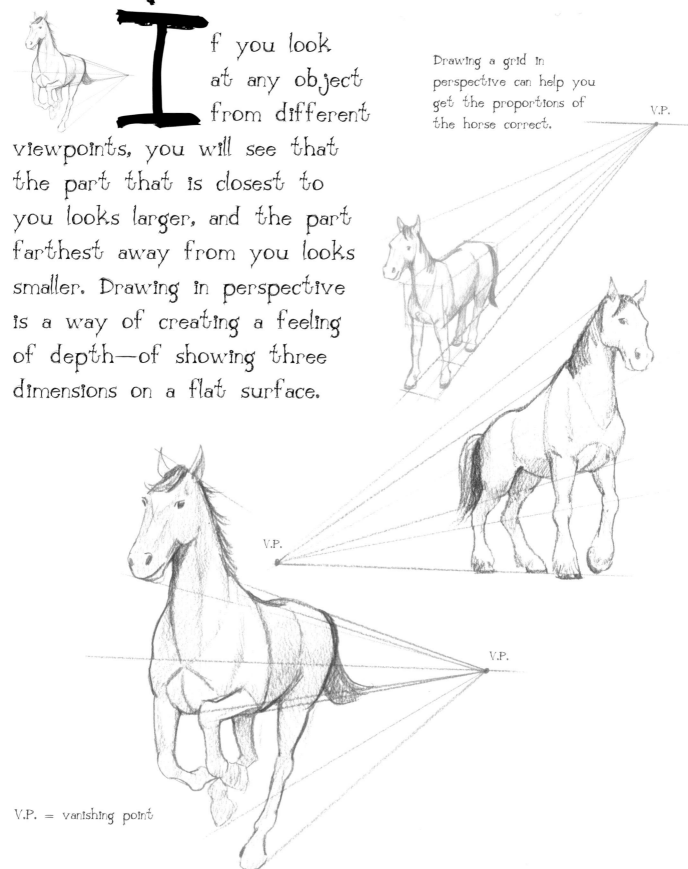

If you look at any object from different viewpoints, you will see that the part that is closest to you looks larger, and the part farthest away from you looks smaller. Drawing in perspective is a way of creating a feeling of depth—of showing three dimensions on a flat surface.

Drawing a grid in perspective can help you get the proportions of the horse correct.

V.P.

V.P.

V.P.

V.P. = vanishing point

The vanishing point (V.P.) is the place in a perspective drawing where parallel lines appear to meet. The position of the vanishing point depends on the viewer's eye level. Sometimes an unusually high or low viewpoint can give your drawing added drama.

V.P.

Think about the relationship between the horse and the horizon line and the vanishing point of the head and legs. This will help you to create a better drawing.

V.P.

11

USING PHOTOS

Drawing from photographs can help you identify shape and form and will help you to draw more accurately.

Choose a good photograph of a horse and trace it.

Mark out a grid over your traced drawing. This will divide your drawing into small sections.

Draw a faint grid of the same proportions on your drawing paper. You can now transfer the shapes from each square of the tracing paper to your drawing paper.

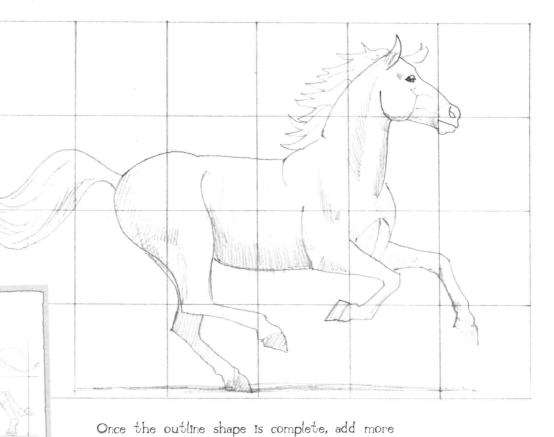

Once the outline shape is complete, add more details to the drawing.

Using the grid

Always refer back to the grid for accuracy. Check each square individually to identify mistakes.

To make your drawing look three-dimensional, decide which side the light is coming from, then add shade and tone to the drawing. Areas where light does not reach should be shaded darker.

Light source

BASIC ANATOMY

These drawings of the front and side views of a horse show the underlying muscle construction. The drawings show the horse's main muscle groups just under the skin. The smaller drawings show how to use light and shade to convey the horse's form.

Light source

Shade areas of the body to show muscles.

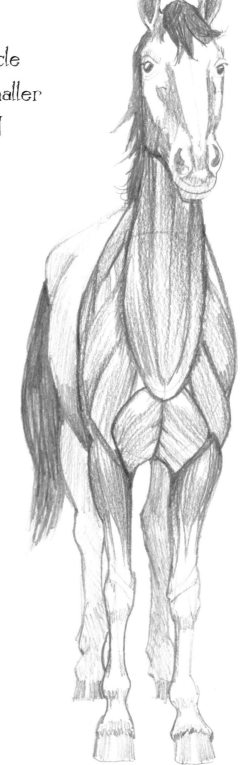

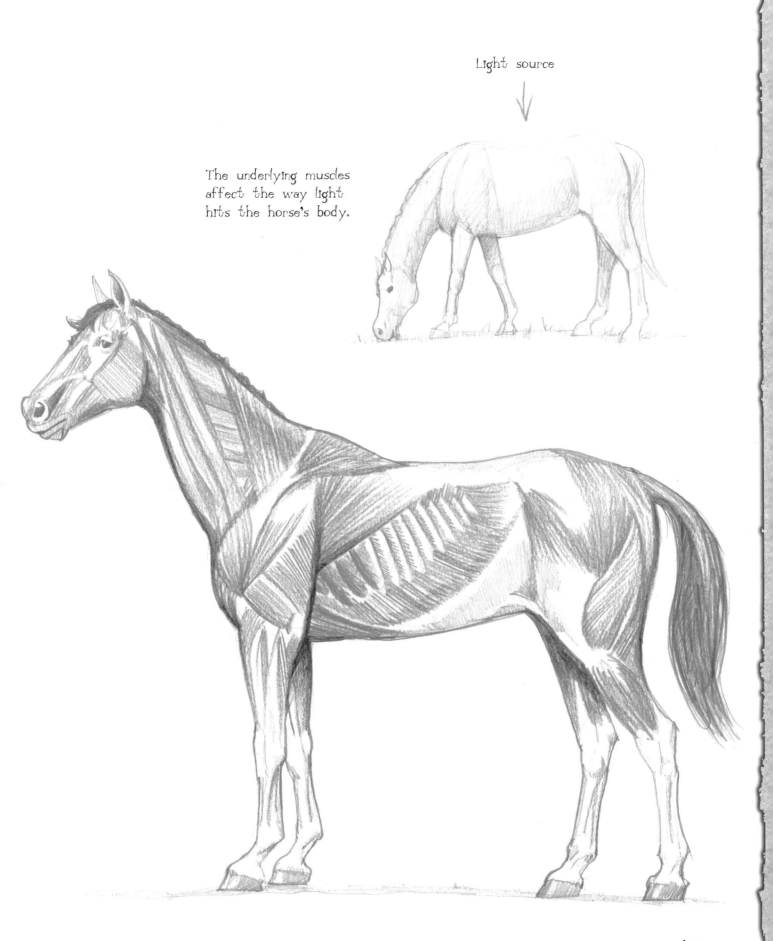

Light source

The underlying muscles affect the way light hits the horse's body.

HEADS AND HOOVES

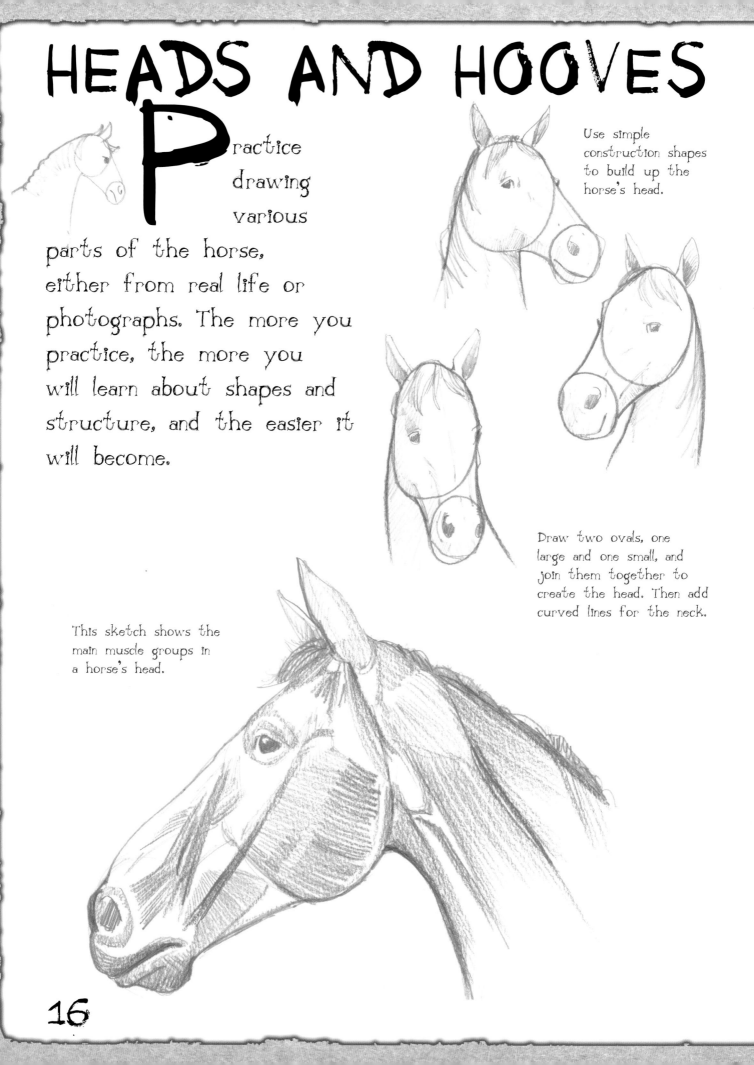

Practice drawing various parts of the horse, either from real life or photographs. The more you practice, the more you will learn about shapes and structure, and the easier it will become.

Use simple construction shapes to build up the horse's head.

Draw two ovals, one large and one small, and join them together to create the head. Then add curved lines for the neck.

This sketch shows the main muscle groups in a horse's head.

The patterns on horse's heads and hooves have names. These are some examples:

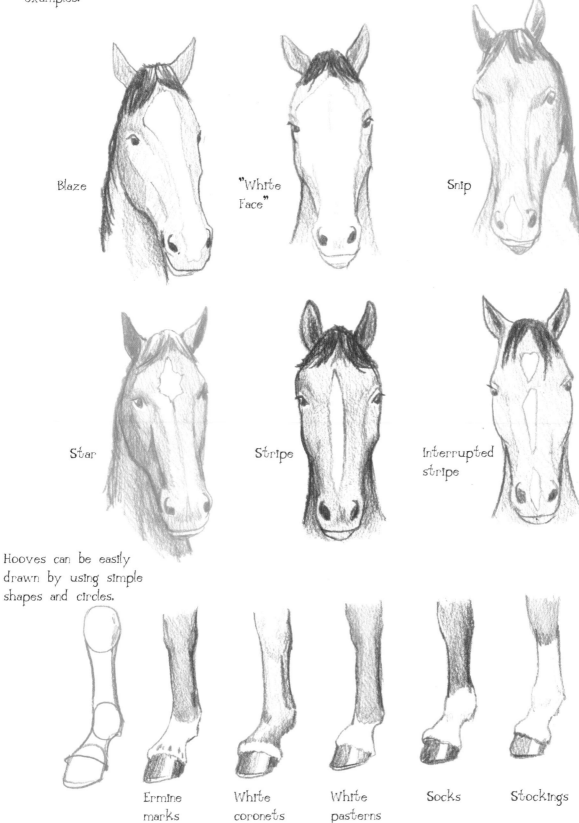

Blaze

"White Face"

Snip

Star

Stripe

Interrupted stripe

Hooves can be easily drawn by using simple shapes and circles.

Ermine marks

White coronets

White pasterns

Socks

Stockings

STANDING POSE

The pictures below are of an Arab horse; probably one of the oldest and most beautiful horse breeds in the world. They are known for having small heads with tapering muzzles. Arab horses have great elegance and almost seem to fly rather than gallop.

Draw two ovals, the front one slightly larger, for the body. Then draw a small circle for the head.

Add curved lines to create the neck and body shape.

Try not to draw these construction lines too heavily, as you may wish to erase some of them later.

Draw in the horse's legs. Use circles for the joints.

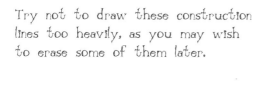

Add the muzzle by drawing a smaller circle and complete the head with two lines.

Add semicircles for the hooves.

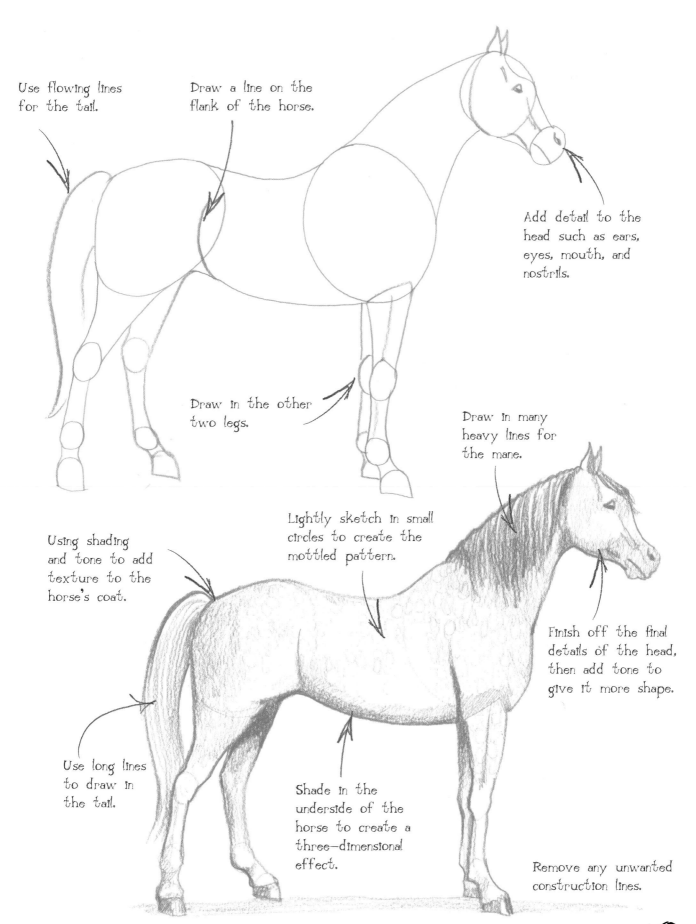

Use flowing lines for the tail.

Draw a line on the flank of the horse.

Add detail to the head such as ears, eyes, mouth, and nostrils.

Draw in the other two legs.

Draw in many heavy lines for the mane.

Using shading and tone to add texture to the horse's coat.

Lightly sketch in small circles to create the mottled pattern.

Finish off the final details of the head, then add tone to give it more shape.

Use long lines to draw in the tail.

Shade in the underside of the horse to create a three-dimensional effect.

Remove any unwanted construction lines.

19

JUMPING

Thoroughbreds have long legs, powerful hindquarters, and graceful necks, which makes them ideal for jumping. Thoroughbred horses compete in both flat racing and "steeplechase," a race that includes jumping over fences.

Draw two ovals for the horse's body and a circle for its head. Join with curved lines to create the shape of the body and neck.

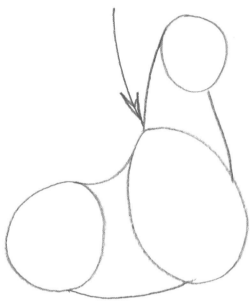

Indicate the shape of the neck with a curved line.

Add the muzzle shape by drawing a smaller circle and complete the head with two lines.

Draw in the legs, using circles for the joints.

Add semicircles for the hooves.

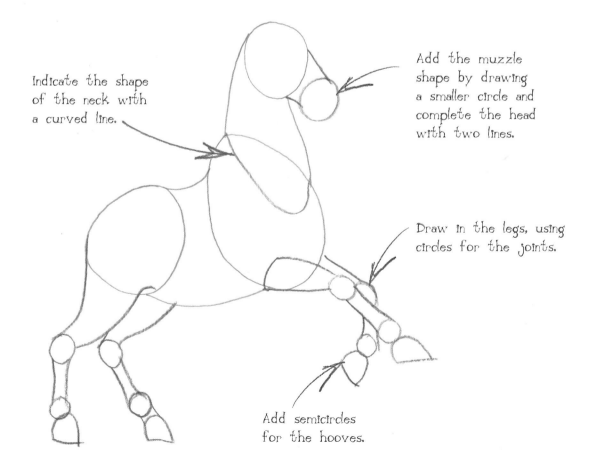

20

Sketch in the eyes, mouth, nostrils, and mane.

Sketch in the flowing shape of the tail.

Add lines to define muscle.

USE A MIRROR
Try looking at your drawing in a mirror. Seeing it in reverse can help you spot mistakes.

Add more detail to the head.

Draw in the mane using jagged backward— flowing lines.

Draw in the tail hair with flowing curved lines.

Shade in those areas of the body that light would not reach. Hatching and cross-hatching are effective techniques.

Add detail and shading to the hooves. Leave an area of white as a highlight.

Remove any unwanted construction lines.

21

GALLOPING HORSE

This breed of horse, a Swedish Warmblood, is very good for jumping and eventing. Swedish Warmbloods are also especially suited to dressage because they are known for their calm demeanor.

Draw two ovals for the horse's body and a circle for the head.

Join up with curving lines to create the shape of the body and neck.

Add the muzzle by drawing a smaller circle and complete the head with two lines.

Draw in the legs, using circles for the joints.

Add semicircles for the hooves.

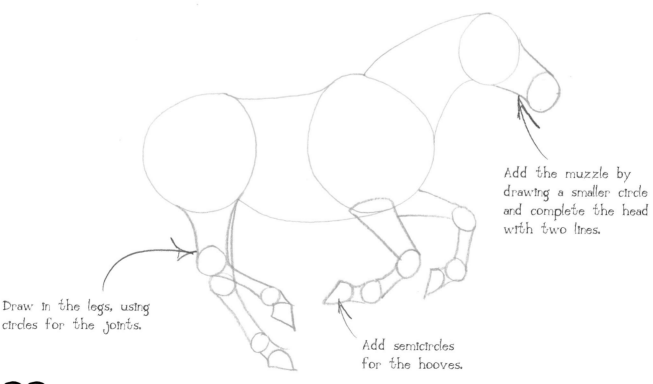

Show the muscle structure, using lines to define the shapes it makes.

Draw in the tail using long flowing lines.

Add detail to the head and draw in a flowing mane.

Add dark areas under the joints.

Add more detail to the mane.

Decide which direction the light is coming from and shade any areas that light would not reach. This will create muscle definition.

Complete the head by finishing off remaining detail and adding tone.

Add shape to the tail with long flowing lines.

Remove any unwanted construction lines.

23

CANTERING HORSE

This horse is the Rocky Mountain breed, one of the newest breeds of horses (registrations began in 1986). Graceful ponies when cantering, they are often chocolate brown and have flaxen manes and tails. This breed of horse can reach speeds of 15 miles per hour (25 kilometers per hour).

Draw two ovals for the horse's body and a circle for its head.

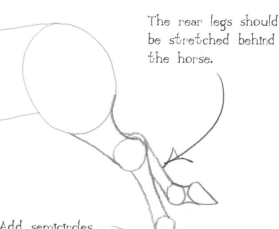

Join these shapes to create the horse's body and neck.

Add the muzzle by drawing a smaller circle and complete the head with two lines.

The rear legs should be stretched behind the horse.

Draw in the legs, using circles for the joints. The front leg should be striding forward.

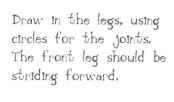

Add semicircles for the hooves.

Use jagged lines for the mane and tail. This gives the impression that the horse is cantering fast.

Add detail to the face. Sketch in the eyes, ears, mouth and nostrils.

Begin to add shading to the horse's body to emphasise the muscles.

Complete all details of the head and mane.

Finish adding tone to create muscle definition.

Add shade to areas of the tail.

Add detail and shading to the hooves. Leave an area of white as a highlight.

Add shade to areas where light wouldn't reach.

Remove any unwanted construction lines.

REARING UP

The Boulonnais horse originally comes from around Boulogne in northeast France. In the past they were used to transport fish from the coastal towns to Paris. They were called mareyeur, which means "fish merchant" in French.

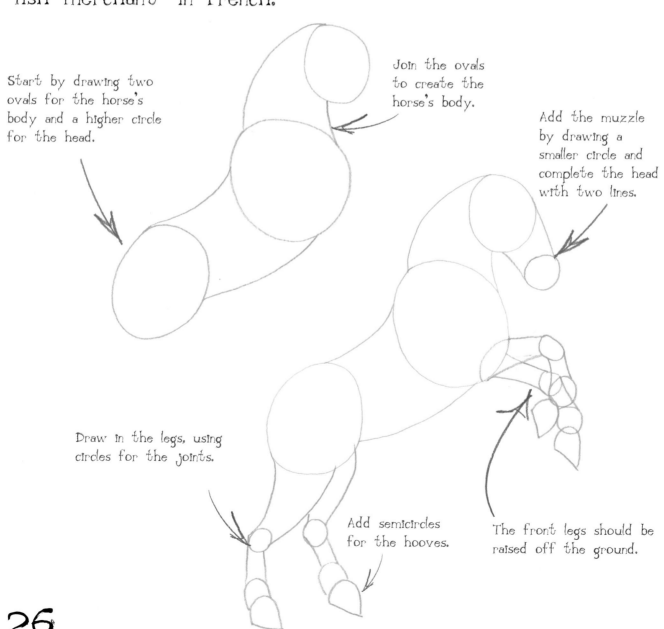

Start by drawing two ovals for the horse's body and a higher circle for the head.

Join the ovals to create the horse's body.

Add the muzzle by drawing a smaller circle and complete the head with two lines.

Draw in the legs, using circles for the joints.

Add semicircles for the hooves.

The front legs should be raised off the ground.

A long, flowing mane gives a sense of movement.

Start to draw in the details of the head.

NEGATIVE SPACE

Look at the shapes left between the lines of your drawing. This can help you spot mistakes.

Sketch in the shape of the tail.

Draw short curved lines for the mane.

Add tone to define the shape of the horse.

Add tone to the hair of the tail.

Add shade to any areas that light wouldn't reach.

Remove any unwanted construction lines.

Add detail and shading to the hooves. Leave an area white as a highlight.

FOALS

The proportions of a foal are very different from those of an adult horse. A foal's legs are longer and its head and eyes are bigger in comparison to its compact body.

Resting foal

Start by sketching two overlapping ovals joined together by two lines to create the body.

Begin adding detail to the head. Draw in a short mane using small strokes.

Draw in the legs, using circles for the joints. In this drawing the foal's legs are tucked underneath.

Draw facial markings to give your foal character.

Draw in two more ovals for the head and muzzle. Add the neck and ears.

Draw in the tail.

Shade in those areas that light would not reach. Hatching and cross-hatching are effective techniques.

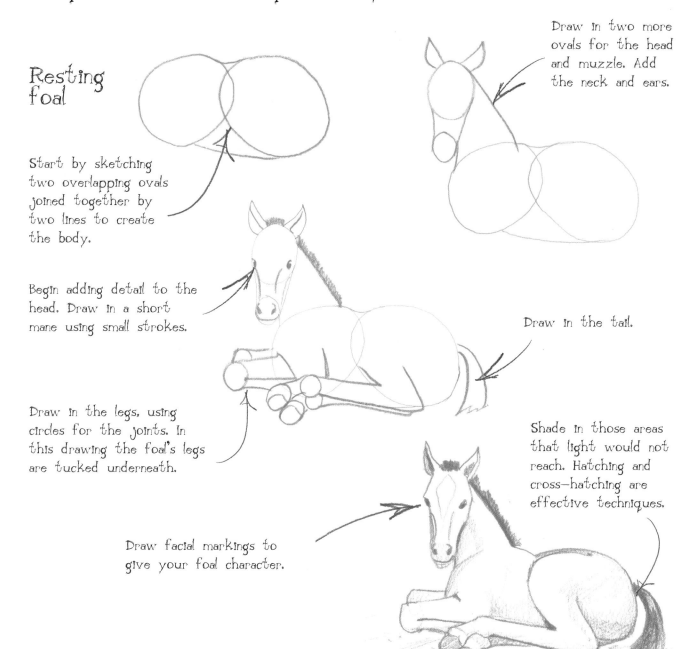

Standing foal

Draw two circles and join them together with two lines.

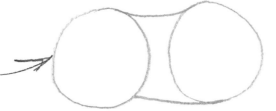

Remember to draw in the construction lines lightly so they can be easily erased later.

Draw a large circle and a smaller circle for the head. Join them together with two lines. Draw in the neck, then add ears.

Use flowing lines to add a short tail.

Begin to add detail to the head.

Add tone to the body to define the foal's shape.

Add shade to any areas that light wouldn't reach.

Draw in the legs, using circles for the joints. Remember that a foal's legs are proportionately longer in comparison to its body than those of a full-grown horse.

Remove any unwanted construction lines.

29

MUSTANGS RUNNING

Mustangs once roamed the plains of the USA. They are descended from horses brought by the Spanish in the 16th century which escaped and became wild. Cowboys and Native Americans used the strong, tough mustangs for cattle herding and transport.

Start by sketching in two overlapping ovals. For the second horse draw two more ovals joined by lines to create the body.

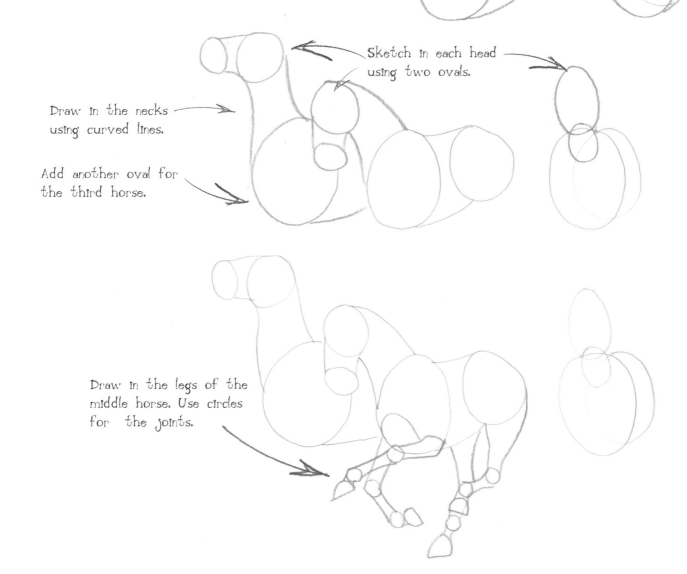

Sketch in each head using two ovals.

Draw in the necks using curved lines.

Add another oval for the third horse.

Draw in the legs of the middle horse. Use circles for the joints.

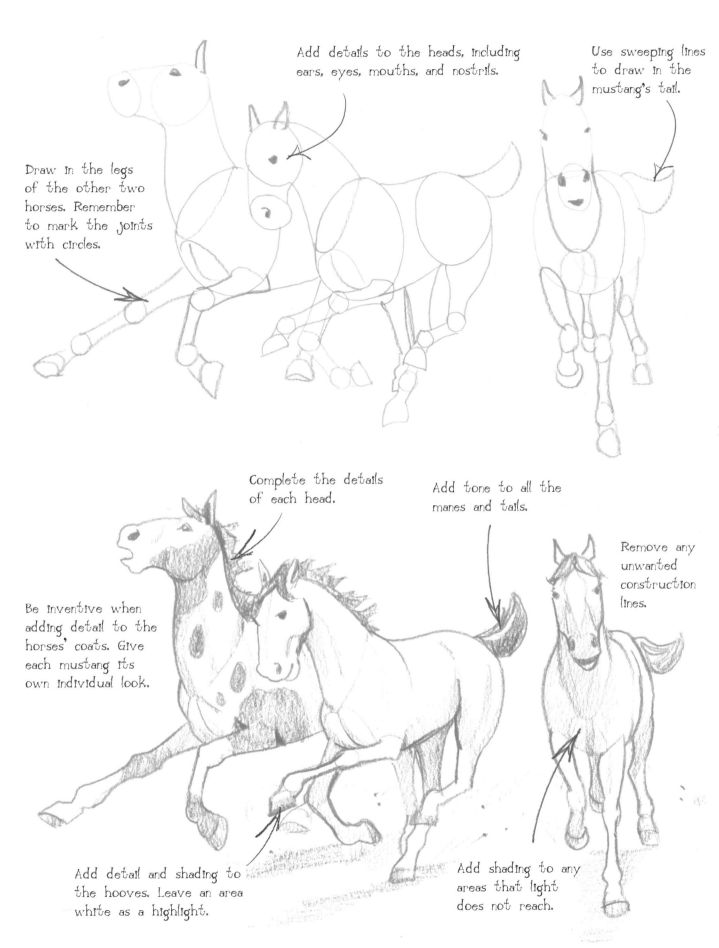

Add details to the heads, including ears, eyes, mouths, and nostrils.

Use sweeping lines to draw in the mustang's tail.

Draw in the legs of the other two horses. Remember to mark the joints with circles.

Complete the details of each head.

Add tone to all the manes and tails.

Remove any unwanted construction lines.

Be inventive when adding detail to the horses' coats. Give each mustang its own individual look.

Add detail and shading to the hooves. Leave an area white as a highlight.

Add shading to any areas that light does not reach.

GLOSSARY

Composition   The arrangement of the various parts of a picture on the drawing paper.

Construction lines   Guidelines used in the early stages of a drawing which are usually erased later.

Cross-hatching   A series of criss-crossing lines used to add dense shade to a drawing.

Hatching   A series of parallel lines used to add shade to a drawing.

Light source   The direction from which the light seems to come in a drawing. Shadows appear on the side of an object which faces away from the light source

Negative space   The area of an image not occupied by shapes or forms. The spaces between shapes can be an important part of the composition in their own right.

Perspective   A method of drawing that gives a realistic imitation of three dimensions.

Silhouette   A drawing that shows only a solid dark shape, like a shadow.

Three-dimensional   Having an effect of depth, so as to look lifelike or real.

Vanishing point   The place in a perspective drawing where parallel lines appear to meet.

INDEX